Home Maintenance Log For:

Address:_____

_____

Date of Purchase:_____

Systems Maintenance By Month

JANUARY

Clean Pipes (Descale overnight)
Clean Showerheads and Taps
Clean and Recaulk Shower/Sinks
Clear Ice Dams In Gutters

FEBRUARY

Deep Clean Oven and Stovetop
Clean Washer
Clean Dyer and Check Vent
Clean Dishwasher & Check Filter

MARCH

Deep Spring Clean
Check Roof for Soft Spots
Check Sump Pump
Clean Gutters

Systems Maintenance By Month

APRIL
Spring Clean Kitchen
Vacuum HVAC Unit
Inspect Attic
Have AC Tuned

MAY
Check Exhaust Fans
Check Ceiling Fan Blades/Dust
Check Weather Stripping
Fix Rust Spots

JUNE
Clean Window Wells
Remove Dead Limbs From Trees
Touchup Paint
Remove Dead Plants From Flowerbeds

Systems Maintenance By Month

JULY
Clean/Stain Deck
Maintain Garage Door
Power Wash Concrete
Check Ductwork for Leaks

AUGUST
Clean Garbage Disposal
Clean Out Freezer
Clean Window Treatments
Change Air Filters

SEPTEMBER
Flush Water Heater
Furnace Tune-Up
Check Pantry for Expired Food
Check Carbon Monoxide Detectors

Systems Maintenance By Month

OCTOBER

- Remove Exterior Hoses & Drain
- Vacuum & Clean Furnace
- Deep Clean Microwave
- Winterize AC

NOVEMBER

- Vacuum Fridge Coils
- Deep Clean Fridge
- Clean Fridge Drain Pan
- Clean Circuit Breakers

DECEMBER

- Test Electrical Outlets
- Run Water in Unused Rooms
- Inspect Fire Extinguishers
- Replace Smoke Detector Batteries

Repairman Contact Information

Company Name:_____
Phone Number:_____
Email:_____
Technician Name:_____

Company Name:_____
Phone Number:_____
Email:_____
Technician Name:_____

Company Name:_____
Phone Number:_____
Email:_____
Technician Name:_____

Company Name:_____
Phone Number:_____
Email:_____
Technician Name:_____

Repairman Contact Information

Company Name:_____
Phone Number:_____
Email:_____
Technician Name:_____

Company Name:_____
Phone Number:_____
Email:_____
Technician Name:_____

Company Name:_____
Phone Number:_____
Email:_____
Technician Name:_____

Company Name:_____
Phone Number:_____
Email:_____
Technician Name:_____

Repairman Contact Information

Company Name:_____
Phone Number:_____
Email:_____
Technician Name:_____

Company Name:_____
Phone Number:_____
Email:_____
Technician Name:_____

Company Name:_____
Phone Number:_____
Email:_____
Technician Name:_____

Company Name:_____
Phone Number:_____
Email:_____
Technician Name:_____

Home Warranty Information:

Company:_____

Premium Paid:_____

Contract Length:_____

Policy Number:_____

Customer Service Number:_____

Online Login User Name:_____

Online Login Password:_____

Appliances Covered:

Refrigerator	
Stove	
Washer	
Dryer	
Dishwasher	
Built-In Microwave	
Trash Compactor	

Ice Maker	
Garbage Disposal	
Other	
Other	
Other	
Other	
Other	

Home Warranty Information (Continued):

Systems Covered:

	Air Conditioning		Central Vac.
	Heating		Septic Pump
	Electrical		Well Pump
	Door Bell		Other
	Smoke Detectors		Other
	Ceiling Fans		Other
	Water Heater		Other

Usage Log:

Date	What Was Serviced	Problem	Service Technician

Home Warranty Information (Continued):

Date	What Was Serviced	Problem	Service Technician

Appliance Information

Date of Purchase	Appliance	Purchased From	Price	Serial Number	Warranty

Appliance Information

Date of Purchase	Appliance	Purchased From	Price	Serial Number	Warranty

Appliance Information

Date of Purchase	Appliance	Purchased From	Price	Serial Number	Warranty

Appliance Repair Log

Date of Service	Appliance	Repairman	Contact Info	Cost	Warranty

Appliance Repair Log

Date of Service	Appliance	Repairman	Contact Info	Cost	Warranty

Appliance Repair Log

Date of Service	Appliance	Repairman	Contact Info	Cost	Warranty

Monthly Maintenance Log

Date	Check Smoke Detectors	Change Furnace Filter	Other:	Other:	Performed By (Initials)

Monthly Maintenance Log

Date	Check Smoke Detectors	Change Furnace Filter	Other:	Other:	Performed By (Initials)

Monthly Maintenance Log

Date	Check Smoke Detectors	Change Furnace Filter	Other:	Other:	Performed By (Initials)

Quarterly Maintenance Log

Date	Check Basement/Crawl Space For Leaks	Clean Fridge	Clean Baseboards	Check Shower/Sink Drain Issues	Performed By (Initials)

Quarterly Maintenance Log

Date	Check Basement/Crawl Space For Leaks	Clean Fridge	Clean Baseboards	Check Shower/Sink Drain Issues	Performed By (Initials)

Quarterly Maintenance Log

Date	Check Basement/Crawl Space For Leaks	Clean Fridge	Clean Baseboards	Check Shower/Sink Drain Issues	Performed By (Initials)

Yearly Maintenance Log

Date	Smoke Detector Batteries	Carbon Monoxide Detector	Clean Gutters	Other:	Other:	Performed By (Initials)

Yearly Maintenance Log

Date	Smoke Detector Batteries	Carbon Monoxide Detector	Clean Gutters	Other:	Other:	Performed By (Initials)

Yearly Maintenance Log

Date	Smoke Detector Batteries	Carbon Monoxide Detector	Clean Gutters	Other:	Other:	Performed By (Initials)

Notes

Notes

Notes

Notes

Notes

Notes

Notes

Notes

Notes

Notes

Notes

Notes

Notes

Notes

Notes

Notes

Notes

Notes

Notes

Notes

Notes

Notes

Notes

Notes

Notes

Notes

Notes

Notes

Notes

Notes

Notes

Notes

Notes

Notes

Notes

Notes

Notes

Notes

Notes

Notes

Notes

Notes

Notes

Notes

Notes

Notes

Notes

Notes

Notes

Notes

Notes

Notes

Notes

Notes

Notes

Notes

Notes

Notes

Notes

Notes

Notes

Notes

Notes

Notes

Notes

Notes

Notes

Notes

Notes

Notes

Notes

Notes

Notes

Notes

Notes

Notes

Notes

Notes

Notes

Notes

Notes

Notes

Notes

Notes

Made in the USA
Las Vegas, NV
29 January 2024